Chapters

CW01455641

1
Run into trouble

Little Ricky Taylor raced round the corner of the school corridor slap-bang into the middle of Nathan's gang.

"Ugh!" gasped Gary, as Ricky thudded into him. "Watch where you're going, you idiot!"

"You're dead right, it *is* an idiot," cackled Nathan. He grabbed hold of Ricky by the back of his jumper. "It's Thicky-Ricky, look!"

"Get off me!" Ricky cried. He struggled free of Nathan's grip, but he was still surrounded by the group of older boys.

"Running away from something, are you?" Nathan sneered. "What have you been up to?"

"Nothing."

"*Nothing!*" Gary scoffed. "He's always running. Trying to run off with somebody's stuff from the cloakroom this time, I bet."

"No, I wasn't," Ricky defended himself. "Leave me alone." The boys jeered.

"Who's gonna believe *you*, Thicky-Ricky?" Nathan taunted him. "You're stupid enough to do anything!"

Ricky spun round, seeking a way to escape, but the gang blocked his every move. Two paintings were knocked off a wall display onto the floor and got trampled.

"Not so fast, kid," said Nathan. "Let's see what you've got in your pockets."

Just at that moment, a teacher's voice bellowed down the corridor.

"What's going on there? Get off outside, the bell hasn't gone yet!"

"It's Jenks," Gary hissed. "Scarper, gang, quick!" Nathan was the last to go.

"You wait!" he warned Ricky. "We'll get you later!"

"You'll have to catch me first," Ricky called after him. Then he hesitated. He had no wish to leave by the same exit, but his class teacher was covering the other.

"Stay there, Ricky, please," called Mr Jenkins. "I'd like a word."

Surprisingly, Ricky obeyed and the teacher strode up before the boy changed his mind. Ricky tended to bolt away when he thought he was in trouble and Mr Jenkins didn't fancy the idea of a chase through the crowded playground to catch him. He'd already tried that once – and failed.

"What was that all about?"

"Nothing," Ricky grunted, looking down at the floor. Mr Jenkins sighed. He hadn't expected any other kind of answer from Ricky.

"I'd stay well out of that Nathan's way in future, if I

were you," he advised. "He's bad news." Ricky blinked. He'd braced himself for another unfair telling-off. "You're not wanting to join that gang, are you?"

Ricky shook his head so fiercely, it was in danger of falling off.

"Good. So what were you doing in here, fooling about with them?"

"I wasn't," Ricky said at last. "They were picking on me. They're always picking on me. Everybody does."

"What for?" asked Mr Jenkins. He was still trying to understand this rather sorry-looking little lad. Although Ricky had been in his class for about three months, the teacher didn't feel that he had got to know him very well yet.

The memory of the headteacher showing the new boy into his classroom one cold, winter morning remained clearly fixed in his mind.

"This is Ricky Taylor, everyone," Mrs Windsor had announced to the Year 5 class of nine and ten year olds. "He's starting at Highgrove School today, and I'd like you all to help Ricky settle in nicely with us here, okay?"

She had tried to sound cheerful, but gave Mr Jenkins a warning glance at the same time. It was as if to say, "This is *him*, the one I told you about. Good luck – you'll probably need it!"

Ricky had stood in the doorway, small and thin, staring blankly at the sea of curious, sniggering faces at the tables. He'd been wearing more or less what he had on now, Mr Jenkins noticed – scuffed trainers, dirty jeans and a ragged jumper with a crumpled T-shirt underneath which looked as though he slept in it, too.

"Well?" Mr Jenkins prompted. "What have people been saying to you?" The boy shrugged and gave in.

"Oh, you know, that I'm scruffy and stupid and everything. Just 'cos I'm titchy, they think I can't stick up for myself..."

Ricky trailed off, deciding he'd said far too much already. It would only make things worse, he reckoned, if others thought he'd been blabbing on them to a teacher.

"I'm sure you can," Mr Jenkins replied, "but it often helps to talk to someone else about any problems too. Are things all right at home?"

The boy's eyes suddenly began to fill up. He turned and fled into the nearby toilet before the teacher could see his tears. Mr Jenkins was cross with himself.

"What a stupid question that was to go and ask!" he muttered under his breath. "Things are never all right at home for that poor little kid."

2
Run out of luck

"You're late again. What time do you call this?"

Ricky didn't answer his mum. He had no idea what the time was. He didn't have a watch. He'd just stayed out, playing on the recreation ground climbing frames until darkness and hunger had driven him home.

He had crept in through the back door, hoping to make himself a quick sandwich without being noticed.

No such luck. One of his kid sisters padded into the kitchen just as Ricky was taking the margarine out of the fridge.

"Mum! He's here!" she yelled out before he could stop her. Mum stood there now in the doorway, arms folded.

"And what have you been doing all this time?"

He shrugged. "Nothing. Just messing about."

"You've been round at your dad's, haven't you?" she accused him.

"No! I don't like going there," he said, honestly.

"Well, that's where your big brother's cleared off to, I bet. And he can stay there, too, as far as I'm concerned."

"Why, what's Scott done?"

"Cheeked me, that's what, so I sent him upstairs."

"Scott went out," his sister piped up. "We heard the door slam."

Ricky pulled a face at her. "I'm hungry," he said.

"You should've been back in time for tea, then," Mum snapped. "I can't hang around here just waiting for you. I've got to go out."

"Where to?"

"Work! Where do you think? I'm working late tonight as well, remember. Could be after midnight again before I get home."

Ricky groaned. He'd forgotten all about that. He hated the neighbour that came round to baby-sit. She did nothing but moan at him.

"What about my tea?" he whined.

"You'll have to go and fetch it. I'm off in a few minutes," Mum told him. She rummaged in her purse for some coins. "Run and get yourself some chips. Go on – and make sure you get back here double-quick."

The door bell rang and Ricky guessed it would be the neighbour. He nipped out into the back yard to avoid her and leant moodily against the wall of the house. A large drop of water plopped onto his head and trickled down his neck.

"Typical!" he muttered. "Now it's starting to rain."

The rain began to slice down from the black sky, bouncing off the dustbins and scraps of metal that had littered the yard since Dad had left. It was more of a rubbish dump than a garden. The only things that grew there were weeds and nettles.

It was tempting to sneak back into the house for his coat, but Ricky was afraid that he might not be able to slip away again. He would rather get wet than be stuck indoors with the bossy neighbour. He wanted to be on his own. He needed time to think. He felt like running.

Running always helped to clear his mind. It had been a bad day, what with the rows at home that morning with Scott and Mum, and then the bullying at school. He had to run everybody out of his system.

He found that running let him escape into a private world of his own, a world that nobody else could share. It didn't matter where he was running to, or what he was running from. Simply running was enough.

Ricky ran hard until he was out of the estate and then settled into a steady jog along the main road. He enjoyed splashing through the puddles that glistened in the bright orange lights overhead. It was only when he reached the shopping area that he halted. Chippie first, he decided, to warm himself up, and then a few sweets.

Ricky gazed through the large windows of the supermarket, past the check-outs, towards the shelves stacked full of bars of chocolate. Suddenly his attention was caught by a familiar figure pushing a trolley along one of the aisles. He could barely believe his eyes.

It was Jenks! It looked so strange to see him out of school, out of place – as if he didn't really belong in the outside world. Ricky stared for longer than he meant to. When the teacher glanced in his direction, Ricky turned away quickly, hoping he hadn't been spotted.

It had stopped raining now and he trotted further on, licking his lips as the mouth-watering smell wafted out from the fish and chip shop. He forgot all about Jenks. All about everything. Life, with a hot bag of vinegar-soaked chips soon burning his hands, was briefly perfect.

Sadly, all too briefly.

As Ricky turned a corner, the bag suddenly exploded up into the air and the chips splattered over the wet, dirty pavement. He was too stunned at first to realize what had happened, but a harsh cackle made him whirl round. His fists clenched.

"Oh dear! Look, lads," Nathan sniggered to his mates. "Thicky-Ricky's gone and dropped all his chips. How clumsy!"

"What did you go and do that for?" Ricky demanded angrily, but he knew there was nothing he could do. There were four of them, all bigger and older than he was.

"Do what?" Nathan gasped, hardly able to speak with laughter.

"Punch my bag of chips like that," Ricky cried.

"Did I? Sorry – my hand must have slipped."

"Oh yeah! You were hiding behind the wall till I came past. That was my tea, that was."

"Ah!" Gary mocked him. "Poor little Ricky's got no tea now. What a shame! He'll never grow up into a big boy if he doesn't eat his tea!"

The gang swaggered noisily away up a side-street and Ricky looked miserably down at the remains of his meal. He kicked at the bag in temper as Nathan called back over his shoulder.

"Told you we'd get you later, Thicky-Ricky. And you said we wouldn't catch you!"

The gang caught him again, too. Although he kept on his guard, Ricky didn't see them double-back on his trail. They followed him into a small general store.

"Fancy meeting you here!" Nathan greeted him. "What a surprise!"

"Clear off, will you!" snarled Ricky.

The shopkeeper did not like the sudden arrival of so many young boys. He danced around behind the counter, trying to keep watch on what all of them were doing in different parts of the store.

"Going to buy us some sweets, are you?" Gary put in.

"Not got enough money."

"That's a pity," smirked Nathan. " 'Cos you're gonna have to pay for all this damage."

"What damage?"

"This damage!"

Nathan pushed Ricky into a nearby display of cans of soft drinks. The pyramid collapsed and the cans crashed to the ground, Ricky sprawling among them.

"Oi!" shouted the shopkeeper. "What d'you think you're doing?"

The gang scrambled outside as the man darted forwards, but Nathan paused at the door.

"It was all his fault, Mister, the titchy one. He did it."

Ricky ducked and dodged around the shelves to escape the man's wild lunges, knocking over some cereal boxes in his panic.

"Come here, you little hooligan!" the shopkeeper shouted in rage, but Ricky was too quick on his feet to be caught. He dashed out of the open door and down the road, relieved there was no sign of any chase.

Just as he reckoned the coast was clear, Ricky ran straight into Mr Jenkins! The teacher was lugging his shopping bags round towards the car park and one of them split open. Tins of beans and soup rolled across the pavement.

"Ricky!" he gasped, starting to scoop up the loose tins. "Always in a hurry. Well, don't just stand there, boy, give me a hand."

"Sorry," Ricky mumbled, out of habit, but he couldn't prevent a chuckle from bubbling out too.

"You don't sound it," Mr Jenkins said, but managed to see the funny side of it himself. "I don't suppose you

expected to bump into me tonight, did you?"

"No, sorry," said Ricky again, handing over the last
of the tins.

"And I didn't expect to be meeting one of my pupils
either, out on their own. About your bed-time, isn't it?"

The boy grinned.

"That's why I was running, like, to get home."

"Hmm," the teacher murmured, unconvinced, but he
stepped aside. "Off you go, then, and make sure you're
on time for school tomorrow morning. You've been late
twice already this week. Good night.

Ricky ran off, taking the first turning out of sight. He didn't see Mr Jenkins call in at the general store to find the shopkeeper tidying up the mess they'd caused.

"Kids today," the man grumbled. "Out of control, they are, most of 'em. Parents don't know where they are half the time."

"Don't know or don't care," Mr Jenkins replied, still thinking of Ricky.

3
Run away

Ricky decided to run away from home.

He knew that Mum would not be back until very late, she'd said so. He reckoned that by the time she discovered he wasn't fast asleep in bed, he could be long gone. He shook his head sadly.

"She probably wouldn't even notice, anyway," he murmured.

Ricky was starving. He'd had no breakfast as usual. Nothing to eat at all that day, in fact, apart from his school dinner. He felt cold, too. He jogged aimlessly around the streets for the best part of an hour, although he lost track of time. He ran until he had chased all doubts clean out of his head. He was definitely going to run away.

He'd tried it once before when his parents split up, but he hadn't got very far. This time it was different.

"Right, they've asked for it," he said under his breath. "I'm going to run away and never come back. Nobody will know where I am – they'll never find me."

He was fed up with being bossed about by

everybody. There'd be no more chores, no more rows, no more school, no more bullies...

Ricky realized with surprise that he must have been running laps of the estate, round and round territory so familiar that he'd been on automatic pilot.

"Might as well see if I can nab some grub from home first before I run away," he told himself. "Get my coat, too."

Only the flickering blue light of the telly showed that anybody was inside the dark house. Gently, he eased the kitchen door open, leaving it ajar for a quick getaway, just in case. He tiptoed across the tiles and shuffled along the gloomy hallway towards the stairs.

His coat was still where he'd slung it in a tantrum that morning, across the bottom steps. At least it saved him a trip up the creaky stairs which might have given him away. He didn't see the shoes on top of his coat. As he lifted the coat, several shoes tumbled down noisily off it.

"Is that you, Ricky?" squawked the neighbour.

"Yes," he called back, hoping she would not leave the lounge.

"About time too. Get yourself off up to bed straight away, I'm watching this programme. And be quiet so you don't wake your sisters."

Ricky was quiet all right. He tugged on his coat, helped himself to some biscuits and a piece of cheese from the kitchen and closed the door silently behind him. He crossed the yard and unlatched the shed. Slumping down between two large boxes, he snuggled inside his coat for warmth, glad to be out of the wind. He nibbled away at the food, his eyelids drooping.

"Think I'll run away tomorrow instead," he murmured sleepily. "Just have a little kip in here for a bit till it gets light..."

Ricky pulled himself stiffly to his feet. He was cold, tired and hungry. The brightness of the early morning sun hurt his eyes as he emerged, blinking, into the yard. The milkman arrived as Ricky came round the front of the house, yawning.

"Up early, aren't you, laddie?" he remarked.

"I'm training," said Ricky, pleased with his quick answer. "You know, off out for a long morning run, like, to keep fit."

The man gave him a wink and moved off, checking back to make sure the boy didn't help himself to anything off his float. Ricky picked up a pint of milk from his own doorstep and took swigs from the bottle as he trotted through the streets. He thought about what he'd said to the nosey milkman.

"Yeah, that's me," he grinned. "I'm a runner, out training for the marathon!"

Ricky tossed the bottle over a hedge as he reached the main road. He ran steadily along the dual carriageway. Soon he was out into the open countryside. He had no idea where he was heading. Just away was enough for now. Far away.

Before long, however, a car slowed down and cruised beside him for a short distance. Ricky ignored it at first, refusing the temptation to look up, but then he gave in. A police car!

A policeman leaned out of the passenger window.

"You're a good little runner," he said, cheerily. "How long can you keep that up for?"

Ricky continued running, head down into the breeze, and the man tried again.

"No school today, then, son? A day off, is it, or are you turning back soon?"

"I'm training," Ricky grunted.

"I see. Does your mum know you're out here by yourself?"

At that point they came to a gate and Ricky suddenly shot off to his left, clambered over it and was away up the field before the police could pull their car off the road onto the grass verge. Ricky had built up a good head start by the time the two police officers stared over the gate in dismay at his disappearing figure.

"I'll hold your jacket for you," the driver laughed. "You're younger than me. Go on, get after him. At the rate that lad's going, he could be in the next county by the time you catch up with him!"

It was a long, sweaty chase for the police constable.

If he hadn't been quite a fit rugby player himself, he might have had to give up. Both he and Ricky stumbled more than once on the rough ground, and they'd climbed over two more gates before he at last clamped his hand on the boy's shoulder in relief.

"Where did you learn to run like that at your age?" the man gasped.

"Nowhere. I just run," Ricky grinned.

"C'mon, let's go and pick up your coat where you dropped it and head back to the car. And walking this time! I need to get my breath back."

"Where will you take me?"

"Back home of course, where you belong."

"I'm not wanted at home," Ricky said sourly as he scooped up his coat. It had nearly landed in a cow pat.

"We guessed there was some kind of problem," the constable sighed. "Your milkman was a bit suspicious and gave us a call. When we woke your mum, she didn't even know your bed hadn't been slept in last night. Where had you been hiding?"

"I wasn't hiding, just dozing for a bit in the shed."

The policeman smiled.

"Thought so. Found some crumbs in there, we did, when we had a quick look round for you. Had much to eat?"

Ricky shook his head and the constable sized the boy up for a few moments.

"OK, tell you what. How about coming down to the police canteen with us first? I need a cuppa and you look as if a nice big cooked breakfast would do you good. How do you like the sound of that?"

Ricky grinned. He liked the sound of that very much indeed.

4
Run off

Over the next few weeks, Ricky's attendance record at school was poor. Some days he turned up, some days he didn't.

He stayed off by pretending to be ill with headaches and feeling sick. He took a whole week off with a slight cold. But when he began playing truant, the school checked up on the reason for any absence.

"He's not here today," Mr Jenkins told Ricky's mum on the telephone. "So if he's not with you either, I'm afraid it looks like he's up to his old tricks."

"Oh no! Not again!" Mrs Taylor wailed. "I got up early as well, to see him off to school, just like the social work lady said I should."

Mr Jenkins sighed.

"Have a look round, if you can, and I'll nip out in my car to see if there's any sign of him. He can't be too far away."

At that moment Ricky was perched on top of a climbing frame on the recky. He'd decided he just couldn't face going to school. Ever since news of his failed attempt to run away had somehow spread, the other kids had been making his life more of a misery.

Ricky yawned and stretched. He'd stayed up very late and hadn't had much sleep. He wished he could go back to bed now, but he guessed Mum would be searching. He jumped down and jogged off towards the shops instead.

While the headteacher took his class, Mr Jenkins drove along the main road for a few miles. Then he made for the shopping centre, thinking of his meeting with the boy there not long ago.

His hunch was correct. There was Ricky sitting on the low wall of the supermarket, tipping crisps into his mouth. Mr Jenkins parked his car and went to sit on the wall nearby. It was a little while before the boy realized who was sitting next to him, and the teacher was glad that Ricky didn't shoot off. He could imagine the scene it would cause if he had to chase him in and out of the shoppers.

"Expected you at school this morning, Ricky," he began. The boy pulled a face.

"Didn't feel like it. Got no friends there. Nobody likes me."

"That's not true."

Ricky shrugged. "Don't care, anyway. I don't like them either. They just make fun of me."

Mr Jenkins knew it was no use arguing any further about that at the moment and changed the subject.

"We've got PE after playtime. You enjoy that, don't you?"

"Ain't got no kit."

"No problem, I'll lend you some – like I normally do."

"Can we go running?" Ricky asked, out of the blue.

"OK, good idea!" Mr Jenkins agreed. "A little run round the field might wake everybody up. Do us all good, including me."

Ricky gave him a cheeky grin. "Race you back to school?"

"No way!" Mr Jenkins choked. "Race you to my car perhaps and we'll go back in comfort. It's just over there. See it?"

Ricky set off immediately, giving the teacher no chance of beating him. He was just relieved that Ricky didn't decide to keep on running.

Unfortunately, even the days when he was at school, Ricky showed no interest in doing any work.

The boy wasn't without ability, Mr Jenkins knew that, but what little written work he did was slow and messy. The only time Ricky perked up was during some science investigations into breathing and pulse rates. He seemed to enjoy running up and down the playground to let others measure how much his rates increased by and how soon they returned to normal. He even drew some graphs of his own performance. But then he spoiled things by tearing the paper up.

He wasted a lot of time as well just fiddling around with pencils and bits of equipment, distracting everyone. He was always getting up from his place and wandering about the room. Mr Jenkins had stopped asking and pretended not to notice. The teacher was trying hard to be understanding, hoping things would improve and that Ricky would eventually settle down.

One afternoon, however, during a games lesson, Mr Jenkins' patience finally snapped.

Ricky borrowed a pair of football boots, but when teams were picked, he was left until last as usual. Nobody wanted him on their side. He tended just to run about all over the pitch, no matter where the ball was. But this time he went into a sulk and the teacher was receiving a stream of complaints from the players.

"Ricky pinched me."

"Ricky scored an own goal deliberately."

"Ricky just came and kicked me on the leg."

Mr Jenkins went over to him.

"Look, I've had enough of all your nonsense. You're not even trying to play properly. Go and run twice round the school field instead."

For the first time that day, Ricky actually smiled and he set off straight away without a murmur.

"That was supposed to be a punishment, not a treat," the teacher said to himself with a frown. He focused his attention again on to the games of five-a-side, but it only seemed a few minutes before Ricky was back with them, barely out of breath.

"I told you to go round *twice*," Mr Jenkins said in irritation.

"I did," Ricky beamed, pleased with himself.

The teacher stared at him.

"You can't have. You haven't had time. You must have cut across the corners or something."

"No, I didn't," the boy protested strongly. "I ran right along the edge all the way."

Mr Jenkins was cross at how Ricky had answered him back.

"I don't believe you. Go and do it all over again to prove it."

As the boy's face fell, the teacher immediately regretted his harsh words, but he felt he couldn't go back on them now. He ordered two boys who were members of his school cross-country squad to shadow Ricky and see that he ran the full course. They were both upset at missing some of their football and took it out on Ricky.

"C'mon, slow-coach, keep up," one of them mocked

him as Ricky trailed moodily behind. "No good now you can't cheat, are you?"

"Cheat! Cheat! Cheat!" chanted the other.

To the watching teacher, Ricky suddenly seemed to speed up at the far side of the playing fields. He smoothly overtook the two boys. Mr Jenkins forgot all about the football going on around him and stared in amazement. He had seen Ricky run many times, but never anything like this. He knew the boy was quick off the mark, but now Ricky was leaving two good cross - country runners far behind him. The gap between them was increasing all the time.

As Ricky came round towards him to complete the first lap, his face was set with determination and pride, though tears were forming streaks down his dirty cheeks.

"OK, Ricky, you can stop now," Mr Jenkins called out. "You've proved your point, well run."

Ricky never even glanced in the teacher's direction, but kept up the same burning pace for the second lap. Mr Jenkins signalled the two flagging lads to pull up.

"Sorry, Mr Jenkins, we couldn't keep up with him," panted the first.

"We were taking the mickey out of him a bit," the second admitted sheepishly, "and he just said, 'I'll show you, I'll show all of you,' and then he burst right past us."

"Doesn't matter," replied Mr Jenkins, gazing at the little figure in the distance. "I think we've all just learnt our lessons regarding Ricky. He *is* showing us. Just look at him run!"

The football had stopped now and all the players began to cheer Ricky on as he entered the last stretch of the course.

"C'mon Ricky, keep it up!" screamed one of them. "Keep going!"

Ricky did just that. He never looked like slowing down as he reached them. He simply continued at full speed over the soccer pitch and clattered across the playground in his studded boots. Mr Jenkins thought he was making for the cloakroom, but Ricky ran straight past it and out of sight round the corner of the building. The pupils looked at their teacher in shock, waiting for him to do something.

"He's run off!" gasped one girl. "Aren't you going after him, Mr Jenkins?" Grim-faced, the teacher shook his head.

"End of game, everyone," he told them. "Get changed while I go and tell Mrs Windsor. There's nothing more I can do about him right now. He's gone."

"Ricky's a good runner, isn't he, Mr Jenkins?" piped up a boy who tagged along beside the teacher back to the school.

"Yes, he is, but I'd never realized before just how good," Mr Jenkins admitted, almost to himself. "I must have been blind."

"The cross-country championships are coming up soon," the boy went on, as if reading the teacher's thoughts. Mr Jenkins nodded and smiled.

"Well, if we ever get Ricky back, I think we can definitely say that he will be 'in the running' now for a place in the team, don't you?"

5
On the run

"My boy was wrong for running off like he did," Ricky's mother told Mr Jenkins the following morning. "But you were to blame as well for showing him up in front of all the other kids."

"I think I was more embarrassed than Ricky," admitted the teacher. "At least everyone saw what a great little runner he can be when he puts his mind to it. He's shot up in their estimation now, I'm sure."

"Good job, too," Mrs Taylor put in. "It was a struggle getting him to come to school today. Had to bring him myself in the end. He thought he was going to be in big trouble, you see."

Ricky hoped his mum would leave, but she kept on talking. "I don't want this place getting like his last school where he was being picked on all the time – by kids and teachers."

"It won't, if I can do anything about it," said Mr Jenkins. "What happened yesterday is forgiven, but not forgotten."

"What do you mean?"

"I mean that the other children won't forget how well he can run – and nor will I," he smiled. "In fact, I'd like him to stay behind after school a couple of times each week to train with my running squad."

"Train? What for?" she asked, as Ricky pricked up his ears.

"For the area cross-country championships. The best runners from all the local schools will be there to race against each other."

"Well, fancy that!" she laughed. "Never knew he had it in him. You think our Ricky is good enough to take part in something like that?"

"I certainly do. What about you, Ricky? Would you like to come along and join our squad?"

The little lad nodded, speechless, his eyes shining with excitement.

"I hoped you would. It will give you a chance to run *for* something at last – for your own good and for the school's – instead of always just running *from* things!"

Ricky actually turned up at school on Friday with his own PE kit, ready for his first training session that afternoon.

"Well done, Ricky," Mr Jenkins greeted him, delighted to be able to praise the boy for being keen. "A good runner should always have his own gear to wear. Trainers OK?"

They both looked down at the things on Ricky's feet. He was wearing his usual old trainers, grubby and torn.

"They're nice and comfy," Ricky said, recognizing that they weren't exactly the smartest pair of shoes in the world. "I'm used to them." The teacher nodded.

"Well, that's the most important thing – comfort. They'll do just fine."

Mr Jenkins seized the rare opportunity, while Ricky was in a good mood, to encourage him to catch up on some work. Not sure how long the "new" Ricky might last, he wanted to try and make the most if it!

Ricky worked harder all day, in fact, than at any time since coming to the school. Perhaps the boy's love of running would begin to rub off in the classroom, Mr Jenkins hoped, and result in some better progress there too. The teacher's hopes were dashed, however, as soon as Ricky reported for training.

The last person Ricky expected to come across in the

cloakroom was Nathan! He felt like he had walked right into a trap. Nathan was there with Gary and several of their mates in Year 6. If Mr Jenkins hadn't been standing in the doorway, collecting valuables, Ricky might well have turned tail and headed for home.

The shock was mutual.

"Well, well, look who it isn't!" Nathan sniggered, loudly enough for Ricky to hear, but not the teacher.

Ricky sat down on the bench among some of the younger boys, trying to ignore further insults. He had been looking forward to this running practice and now it was completely spoilt.

"Don't leave any money lying about, lads, or it'll get nicked," Nathan said, to taunt him. Ricky jumped to his feet.

"That's not fair. I'm no thief."

"Why were you on the run from the police, then?" he sneered.

That was too much. Ricky flew at Nathan, but he was blocked by the other boys just as Mr Jenkins came to see what all the noise was about.

"He started it," Nathan said cockily, pointing at Ricky. "I was just minding my own business, getting changed, and he went for me."

Mr Jenkins was not taken in by Nathan. As far as the teacher was concerned, there were two things that Nathan was very good at. One was running and the other was causing trouble.

"There's no need for any rivalry between you at cross-country," he told them both. "The area races are in different age groups, so you're not having to try and beat each other to get in the team."

"Huh!" grunted Nathan as Ricky was led off to the other side of the room. "As if a little titch like that stood any chance of beating us."

"Yeah," Gary agreed. "He'll be miles behind."

Nathan nudged him. "And we'll make sure that he

is, eh, pal?"

Mr Jenkins could have kicked himself for forgetting about Nathan. The boy didn't always bother to turn up for practices and the teacher doubted whether he would pick him for the championships. Nathan's ability did not make up for his nasty behaviour towards the other children.

He could only hope that Ricky hadn't been put off, but he feared the worst. Ricky had already gone into one of his sulks.

"Not a good start," the teacher muttered as he went outside to organize the warm-up exercises.

It wasn't a good start at all. The squad of boys and girls from Years 4, 5 and 6 set off in a big bunch together, but they had not gone thirty metres before Ricky found himself flat on his face. In the tangle of legs and bodies, he had been tripped up from behind.

He didn't see who had done it, but knew it wasn't an accident. As he picked himself up and trundled after the pack ahead of him, Ricky could hear Nathan's cackling laugh.

As the runners spread out into a long, thin line, Ricky was too upset to make any real effort to catch up with the leaders. They were mostly from Year 6, with Nathan and Gary among them. He just dawdled along somewhere in the middle instead.

Mr Jenkins jogged around inside the large playing fields to keep an eye on all the children. Not everyone at the practice would be chosen for the area teams, but he was just as interested in the performance of those at the back as the ones up nearer the front.

He was disappointed to see Ricky lagging behind, though. He hadn't noticed Ricky's fall. He just thought Ricky must still be sulking. The teacher realized it would perhaps be a bit of a gamble to select him after all. The boy could be so moody, they might not be able to rely upon him to do his best. He ran over to have a quick word.

"How are you feeling, Ricky?"

"All right," he mumbled.

"Can you go any faster?"

"If I wanted to."

"Well, let me see you put in a good, strong sprint finish, OK?"

But it was clear that Ricky was keeping a lot in reserve. After the youngest runners finished their laps, Mr Jenkins signalled the Year 5 athletes to stop as well. Ricky was about the only one of them who didn't seem out of breath. He even ran back to the cloakroom while the others walked.

By the time Mr Jenkins returned with the Year 6 group a little while later, Ricky was gone. So, Nathan claimed, was his watch.

"And we all know who's nicked it, don't we?" he cried.

Mr Jenkins was furious with Nathan. "You can't go blaming somebody just like that without proof. If we can't find the watch anywhere now, we'll check with people about it on Monday."

As Nathan searched half-heartedly on the floor, he hissed to Gary, "We'll sort that little thief out, eh, before Monday – in our own way!"

6
Run free

It was Saturday evening when Nathan and his gang spotted Ricky on his own on the recky's apparatus. The four boys closed in, sneaking along the hedge.

By the time Ricky was aware of them, it was too late. He was on top of a wooden frame and decided to stay up there.

"What do you want?" he demanded, from his perch.

"I want my watch back that you nicked," shouted Nathan.

"What watch?"

"Hear that? Reckons he knows nothing about it," Gary laughed. "And knowing him, he's probably daft enough to be wearing it."

"Right, let's find out," said Nathan. "And this time there's no Jenks to come and spoil our fun. Go get him, gang."

Nathan remained on the ground while the other three began to scramble up the ladders and bars to force Ricky off. But they reckoned without his speed and gymnastic skills. He had practised for many long hours on these frames. He knew all the different layouts upside-down!

Ricky waited until the last second and then leapt daringly through the air to grab hold of a rope that hung down from a mast-like pole. He swung round and kicked out at Nathan as the bully unwisely got too close to his flailing feet.

Ricky missed, but it made Nathan more wary. He kept well out of range after that, allowing Ricky to drop off the rope and run over to balance on another high platform.

"You can't get away," Nathan cried. "We've got you trapped here!"

"Come and catch me, then," Ricky challenged, laughing in excitement.

They certainly tried, but Ricky was as nimble as a monkey. He scampered across and up and along one piece of apparatus after another, just keeping out of reach of grasping hands. He made his final escape by hurling himself, head first, down a chute. He slid down so fast that the boy at the bottom was too slow to move out of the way and gave Ricky a soft landing – right into his tummy!

Ricky saw his chance and was off, racing towards the recky gates. Only two of the gang, Nathan and Gary, were in the cross-country squad and the other two didn't have the stamina to run hard over a long distance. They soon dropped out of the hunt, but Ricky's lead began to be cut back as Nathan and Gary tore after him through the streets.

Ricky stayed calm, knowing he had one more spurt left in him to reach home. He slowed slightly, letting Nathan and Gary close the gap even more. Then his sudden burst of extra speed took his chasers by surprise. The older boys were already at top speed and could not believe it when they saw Ricky pulling further away from them. They staggered to a halt, puffing and blowing, and shook their fists in vain at the fast-disappearing Ricky.

At school on Monday, Ricky denied taking Nathan's watch. Mr Jenkins had never expected him to admit anything, of course, but he liked to believe that Ricky was probably telling the truth.

Something, he felt, was not quite right about this whole business. It had been niggling away at the back of the teacher's mind all weekend. When a child asked him what the time was during the lunch break, it finally hit him. He sent for Nathan to come to his room.

"I've been thinking about this watch of yours," he

began when Nathan arrived, hands in pockets. "When I was collecting people's valuables, why didn't you give it in to me like the others did?"

"Oh, just forgot," Nathan said casually.

"Pity. It would have saved all this fuss."

"Yeah, guess so. But it shows that Ricky's a thief and liar."

"Does it? Have we found the watch on him, then?"

"Well, no, not yet."

"No, and I don't suppose we ever will now. I'm going to ring your mother up and apologize for the fact that your watch was stolen."

Nathan went pale. "Er, no, I've already told her," he gabbled in alarm. "There's no need to bother."

"Oh, no bother at all, Nathan. I think it's best if it came from me too, as I feel responsible in a way."

Nathan panicked, falling over a chair as he tried to stop the teacher making for the door.

"No, wait, Mr Jenkins, er, she's not in. She always goes out shopping at this time."

"How do you know what time it is, Nathan? You haven't got a watch."

"No, but..."

"The thing is, Nathan," the teacher said quietly, "I can't remember you *ever* handing a watch in to me for safe keeping. You never wear one, do you? In fact, I'm wondering if you even own a watch at all..."

The boy hung his head in shame and said nothing.

Mr Jenkins sighed. "Now who's been telling lies, Nathan?"

The headteacher, Mrs Windsor, suspended Nathan from school for a week for trying to get another pupil into serious trouble. He was also banned from taking part in any more sports activities for Highgrove.

Nathan was out of the area championships! After what had happened, Mr Jenkins had no intention of choosing him anyway.

The news of Nathan's punishment soon spread around the school. So, too, did the tale Gary told about Ricky's great escape act from the gang. As a result, Ricky was amazed at how much friendlier the other children became towards him all of a sudden.

At the next cross country-practice, Gary wanted to make friends too.

"Sorry for everything, Ricky," he began. "You needn't worry about the gang any more. It's broken up. We're finished with that Nathan. We had no idea he was making it all up about the watch – honest!"

Ricky grinned.

"Forget it. Let's just go out and run, OK?"

"Yeah," said Gary in relief, then added, "So long as I don't have to chase you again. You're too quick for me."

Ricky proved too quick for everyone except Aniz in Year 6, the school's best athlete. But at the squad's final practice session a week later Ricky even managed to outpace him as well!

Ricky was the first name Mr Jenkins read out as he announced the Year 5 team for Saturday's area championships and he glanced up to enjoy the boy's reaction. Ricky's mouth hung open, as if he couldn't believe he had really been chosen.

"Gobsmacked!" was how Ricky described himself later when Mr Jenkins spoke to him.

"You have a natural talent for running, Ricky, a very special talent – and one that mustn't be wasted. Do you realize that?"

Ricky gave his usual shrug, but this time it was through shyness at receiving the kind of praise he'd never had before.

"Dunno, I just run," he said.

Mr Jenkins smiled. "You certainly do – with tremendous speed and stamina. You're our star cross-country runner now, and all the other children know that too."

Ricky grinned, embarrassed, before a dark cloud seemed to pass over his face.

"What's the matter?" Mr Jenkins asked.

"Oh, it's just that Dad always said I was a useless little good-for-nothing," Ricky sighed, and then chuckled. "I used to think he was right as well – but at least now I've found out I can be good at something!"

7
Keep on running

"Are you sure you've done the right thing, picking Ricky?"

The headteacher was standing outside the school on Saturday morning, with Mr Jenkins, waiting for all the runners to arrive. They were travelling by coach together, but there was no sign yet of Ricky.

"No, I'm not sure – but hopeful," he replied, truthfully. "Ricky's attitude has changed a lot since he took up cross-country. He's trying much harder in class now. I don't think he'll let us down."

"So where is he?" asked Mrs Windsor.

Mr Jenkins checked his watch nervously. "If he's not here soon, I'll drive round to his house to find out what's going on," he said. "It's a struggle for Mrs Taylor to cope with all that family of hers. She's given up her evening job so she can be with them more, and at least she seems to be trying her best with the boy."

"Hmm, I wish I could share your faith in him."

"You will, when you see how he can run."

"*If* I do, you mean…" Mrs Windsor left the sentence unfinished as a police car pulled into the school. There in the passenger seat sat Ricky Taylor.

"Oh, my goodness!" she gasped. "What's he done now?"

Ricky was grinning broadly, however, as he jumped out of the car. He was soon surrounded by the other runners, eager to hear about this latest adventure. The local police constable, too, was all smiles.

"Don't worry, nothing wrong. Came across him by the shops, dashing around in a flap, running errands for his mum. He was worried about being late for school – on a Saturday!"

"My word!" Mrs Windsor laughed. "Ricky *has* changed!"

"When he told me about the cross-country, I said I'd run him up to school," the policeman went on. "And, d'you know, he refused at first. He thought I meant giving him a race, not offering him a lift!"

"Must be the only time in his life he didn't want to run anywhere!" chuckled Mr Jenkins. "Perhaps he's trying to save his energy."

"Well, let's hope he's got enough left for the big race," said the policeman. "It'd be a great confidence boost for the lad if he won."

"Fingers crossed. Thanks for your help."

"All in a day's work," he grinned. "I even took Ricky home with the shopping. His mum nearly had a fit when she saw me turn up again!"

"Serves her right!" the headteacher put in. "Fancy sending Ricky out to the shops like that, today of all days!"

Mr Jenkins shook his head. "I don't know, maybe it will show her how much this really means to Ricky," he said, and then called out to the runners, "Right, everybody's here, let's go. All aboard!"

The area championships opened with two Year 4 races, and the youngest Highgrove boys and girls gave the school a good start with several top-ten places.

Ricky watched the next race for Year 5 girls with keen interest, too, cheering on a classmate who finished runner-up. He'd also been checking out the course around the large public park where the competition was being held. There was a hilly part up towards a small wood and the narrow trackway through the trees, he noticed, was quite rough.

His own race was over two laps of the course and Ricky was impatient to hear the starter's gun. He could hardly wait to set off running.

"I'm really going to charge up that hill," he decided.

"Your turn now at last, Ricky, this is it," said Mr Jenkins. "Give it all you've got. Do you feel on good form?"

Ricky nodded. "I'll pretend that copper's chasing me. That'll make me run fast."

Mr Jenkins laughed. "Run well today, and the only thing he'll be after you for in the future is your autograph!"

Ricky kept out of the crush at the start as best he could, just managing to avoid one boy who slipped and fell in front of him. But after the hectic free-for-all, the runners soon found their own rhythm, with Ricky among the leading group. They tackled the hill almost in single file and Ricky was the only one to do any overtaking. As the others slowed their pace, he moved strongly up into fifth position.

He had always taken his running for granted before as just something he enjoyed doing. But now he knew he could actually do it better than most other people, it made him feel good. He felt in control.

Ricky loped through the wood, shoulder to shoulder with another boy and then swept past him going downhill again. He even had time to flash Mrs Windsor a cheeky grin as he sped along in front of the main group of excited spectators to complete the first lap.

"Run, Ricky, run!" shouted the headteacher. "Keep it up!"

"You're going great!" yelled Mr Jenkins, but then he groaned. A boy behind Ricky made a desperate, clumsy effort to pass him as they ran round a bend and his foot accidentally caught the back of Ricky's heel, yanking off his trainer.

Ricky was knocked off balance, and the boy seized his lucky chance to squeeze past as Ricky hobbled along for a short way on one shoe. He never even thought of turning back to find the lost trainer. He just ripped off the other as well and carried on in his socks. But that was no good – they didn't have enough grip – so he pulled the socks off too and tossed them away. He would have to finish the race barefoot!

It felt very strange at first, but the course was mostly well grassed and not too hard. What his handicap did do was make Ricky even more determined, and he pressed on hard to try and close the gap again.

Mr Jenkins cut across the inside of the roped-off course to shout encouragement.

"You can still do it! Go on, Ricky, run for it!"

Many of the other Highgrove runners were also trying to scurry around the course to cheer Ricky on. Gary was among them.

"C'mon, Ricky!" he screamed. "Win! Win! Win! Shut Nathan up for good!"

That was the final spur Ricky needed. He pushed on harder, his bare feet giving him a feeling of extra freedom, like running on the beach. He came up level again with the boy in fourth place who was tiring badly.

The runner glanced to one side and recognized Ricky. "Sorry..." he panted. "... Your shoe."

"Forget it," Ricky replied, and as they came to the hill, Ricky left him for dead. He stormed up it at full power, catching the third place boy as well totally by surprise. Now there were only two people ahead of him and he hurtled after them into the shade of the woodland track.

As they broke out of the trees again into the spring sunshine, the Highgrove supporters saw Ricky was now in the middle of the front trio. What they didn't know was that one of his feet was bleeding.

He'd caught his toes on a twig in the wood as he veered wide to take second spot, but he still galloped down the slope. And when he saw the finishing line in the distance, it made him forget all about his foot. Ricky had only one thought fixed in his mind – winning the race.

The leader sensed Ricky was coming, heard his breathing and glanced round in panic. He'd felt he was going to win the race himself, but the sight of little Ricky pounding up right behind him made his heart sink. He tried to respond, to find more strength, but he knew it was no use.

Ricky produced that same scorching burst of speed

that had shaken off Nathan and Gary. He ate up the ground as fast as a sprinter and surged past the boy with only twenty metres left to go.

There would be no catching Ricky now. His rival had to settle for being runner-up, as Ricky zipped past the cheering crowd to break through the tape at the finish. It was the best moment of his whole life. He was Area Champion!

"Fantastic! What a run!" Mr Jenkins enthused, giving Ricky back his shoes and socks. "You took your big chance with both hands today."

"With both feet, you mean – and bare ones at that," Mrs Windsor chuckled, sitting Ricky down to attend to his cuts. "Well done, young man, we're all very proud of you."

"We sure are," came a voice from behind them.

"Mum!" cried Ricky. "I didn't know you were coming."

"Neither did I!" she laughed. "Jumped on a bus at the last minute. I reckoned I should try to make up for that mix-up at home this morning by being here myself to see how you got on. Glad I was – else I might not have believed it! Do you want to be a runner, then?"

Ricky couldn't stop grinning, he felt so happy. But he thought it was a bit of a funny question to ask.

"I already am," was all he could say in reply.

Thanks to Ricky's victory and two other high placings by his team-mates, Highgrove won the Year 5 boys' trophy. And they almost claimed the main prize too for the best school performance in the championships.

Aniz had also finished first, as expected, in his Year 6 race, with Gary fifth, following excellent efforts by the older girls. But in the end, when the points scored during the whole morning were added up by the judges, Highgrove just came second overall.

"You've qualified to run in the major county championships next month now," Mr Jenkins told Ricky, after he had received his own winner's certificate. "Who knows, with a bit of luck, you might even be able to go and win there as well!"

A few minutes later Ricky stepped forward again, this time on behalf of the school, to be presented with the trophy. He held it high in the air, shyly at first, and then lapping up all the loud applause. He saw Mum at the back of the crowd, waving madly at him.

Soon he was off, running again, leading the rest of the squad around part of the course. The children ran and danced along, passing the cup from one to another to celebrate their success.

"That's right, Ricky, make the most of it," Mr Jenkins murmured to himself in pleasure as he watched. "It's not every day that you're a hero. Just keep on running!"